Realize the Blessing

To start, I need to tell you about my disability which is
Cerebral Palsy and that I have been confined to a
wheelchair my whole life. The disability itself has many
different forms, some of which include the ability to walk
and/or talk, as well as sometimes cognitively. Cerebral
Palsy occurs at the time of birth. In my case, the umbilical
cord was wrapped around my neck which cut off the
oxygen to my brain. Thank goodness it didn't hamper my
good looks. As a result, all four of my extremities were
affected. Considering that, I am so thankful that it did not
affect my cognitive ability. Consequently, I have been
blessed with a mind that is extremely sharp despite my
severe physical limitations. I do realize that there are
people out there with the same type of disability and are
not as fortunate. Therefore, my goal is to honor them to the
best of my ability. Even more so, to be a pioneer for those

who come after myself to show that anything can be accomplished with ingenuity, creativity and determination and having the loving support of family and God.

The motivation behind writing this book is for several reasons. First, I believe over the last 10-15 years the culture of America has changed. By this, I mean we have established a society of negativity where this has become the "new normal." In America, we have chosen to make a conscious effort to look at the glass as being half-empty with entitlements. Additionally, our society has chosen to take on this type of attitude which allows one to not take full responsibility for oneself or their actions. In turn, the individual misses out on all the endless opportunities which are right in front of them to grow and prosper. By taking on this attitude, individuals are going to surround themselves with people of the same mindset. This is extremely self-centered, outwardly wrong and totally disregards that life itself is a gift which should not be taken for granted! I firmly believe that every single day is a brand-new day and I have a personal choice to embrace it with all that is good and to face the challenges head-on with a positive attitude. Life presents us with a choice and what we decide to do with that choice is up to everyone. I am not saying that throughout this journey life has not been difficult at times. I have had to make some major adjustments along the way, some easy and some not so easy. Through all of this I have come to the realization that my disability is a part of me and a part of life's journey.

In beginning to write my autobiography, I've decided to start off with just some random thoughts. That is not to say that there are times when I am reminded of my disability when it smacks me right square in the face. When those situations have occurred, I have come to understand that it is a part of life and that "this too shall pass." Later on in this memoir, I will share more of the struggles and barriers that I have overcome. Through the years, I have come to the realization that I am very blessed. In this storybook, I will give you numerous examples of how God has blessed me and guided every footstep.

The first story that I recall was the Summer 1971, when my father, Jim Mueller, was able to contact the general manager, Carroll Rosenbloom, for the Baltimore Colts and explained that his son was a real fan of the football team. That summer, the Colts were practicing in Golden, Colorado, for several days I believe at Regis College. My father requested that myself and my brother, Todd, would be able to see their team practice. Mr. Rosenbloom went one step farther and invited us to go on the field to watch the team practice. What an amazing time for a 13-year-old boy! After practice, Mr. Rosenbloom then asked us which players we wanted to see. Without hesitation, I responded, "Johnny Unitas, Tom Mattie and Earl Morrell", and my wish came true! That will be something I will never forget. I can remember my father using a Kodak instamatic camera and Johnny signing a piece of paper, when my father yelled "Hey Johnny" and Mr. Unitas looked up at my father taking some pictures. To this day, 55 years later, I still have this captured moment on display in my house.

The second story I recall was in 1974, when the Denver Nuggets hired Larry Brown to be the head coach. They also hired Doug Moe as the assistant coach, and Carl Scheer to be the general manager. The year before that season, Larry Brown was the head coach for the Carolina Cougars of the American Basketball Association (ABA). Denver was also part of the ABA. In the Summer of 1974, the Nuggets had just drafted Bobby Jones from the University of North Carolina, and Jan Van Breda Kolff from the University of Vanderbilt. On one particular day, I believe it was in July, the Nuggets offered a mini clinic at the University Hills Shopping Center in Southeast Denver, near my house. At one point during the clinic, they had a free throw shooting contest, and my brother, Todd, hit 10 free throws in a row. Doug Moe came back with a statement saying, "Who is his agent?" At that time, I spoke up, and without hesitation stated, "I am." I can remember

Doug Moe turning around to see who said that, and here was this boy in a wheelchair, catching his eye. I can remember he kind of chuckled at that remark. After the clinic was over, there was an opportunity to get some autographs, and I introduced myself to Larry Brown. At this point, I told Larry that picking up Bobby Jones and Jan Van Breda Kloff, along with two veteran guards, Mack Calvin and Lionel "Fatty" Taylor, were great additions to the squad. I can remember that they were going to play the Boston Celtics in two exhibition games. As the story continued, I told Larry that they would take two games from the Boston Celtics. His response was "We will be lucky to take one". Well, as it turned out, they ended up winning both games. A month later, there was an autograph session scheduled before a regular-season game, and I went up to "Fatty" Taylor for an autograph and he said, "You are the one who said we would take two from Boston." As the season went on, the relationships with Larry and Carl Scheer continued to grow into very close friendship between these two gentlemen. Periodically, then down Larry would make an appearance on the radio called Sports Talk on 850 AM radio in Denver, Colorado. Whenever Larry was a guest, I would call him on the radio to ask a question. Larry would automatically recognize my voice and say, "how you doing, Tracy?" The talk show host, Mr. Bob Martin, was probably thinking to himself who is this guy? Larry would also give me his personal phone number and I would just call to chat. However, almost every time I would call, he would offer me tickets to a game. On one occasion, Larry bought me tickets to a playoff game against the Kentucky Colonels, who at the time had Artis Gilmore at center. My seats were right at center court at McNichols Sports Arena, about five rows back, and I was sitting next to Larry Brown's wife, Barbara, and Carl Scheer's wife, Marsha. Before McNichols Sports Arena was built, they used to play at the Denver Auditorium Arena [which holds about 7, 700] and I used to go into the locker room almost after every game. I can remember both of my brothers Todd and Troy, hanging on to my shirttails, being in total awe of the situation.

Several years later, my brother, Todd was playing organized basketball at the Schlessman YMCA in Southeast Denver. My father came home one Saturday afternoon after registering my brother to play. I came up with the idea of helping my father coach the team. Now you need to understand that my brother was very athletic in both basketball and baseball. My father was also very smart in teaching how to play the game. More specifically, my father would teach the very fundamentals of how to play on the defensive side of the ball. To this day, my memory recalls him teaching either closing off the baseline or trapping along the baseline. He also taught my brother how to shoot a turnaround jumper. This shot was virtually undefendable, and my brother could hit it from anywhere in the forecourt. After several years as my father's assistant coach, we somehow switched roles. However, in reality, my father was still the head coach. I can remember thinking to myself, even though I could not play the game, I could still participate and learn the mental aspects of the game. At this point I want to share another story. One day my father and I were heading to a game and as my father was taking my wheelchair down a flight of stairs, a kid probably five or six years old was going up stairs. The boy stopped in the middle of stairs and asked me why I was in a wheelchair. I responded and stated that "I was born this way." The boy responded and said "You were born in a wheelchair." My dad began to laugh so hard that he almost lost me down a flight of stairs. On a different note, my brother Todd has taught me so much how to analyze football, basketball and baseball. To be honest with you, I am still learning more about the sport of baseball from my brother. Over the years, Todid has taught me how to think analytically in that area. This has also carried over into real life. More specifically, I can see his genuine concern for people and their overall well-being. One of my recent goals is to continue coaching at a high school, have fun, and to be a mentor for the youth of the future.

Growing up, my parents were absolutely amazing. They took a special interest in my brother's activities as well as myself. Looking back, once my parents realized that their oldest son had a disability, I would think their reaction would be a sense of disappointment, fear and a lot of questions. However, they both knew intrinsically and by their strong Christian faith that their son was very special and deserved every opportunity that life has to offer. My mother was especially gifted in this area, especially in the beginning of my educational years. I can remember my mother telling me the story of going to Children's Hospital in downtown Denver and how a physical therapist took a special interest in me. I remember the person, her name was Ellie Guilfoyle. Anyway, in this story, my mother told me how on one occasion, I was given an IQ test and I was instructed to match the square blocks in the proper location. Well, naturally, with the limited mobility due to cerebral palsy, I had difficulty performing certain tasks. However, Ms. Guilfoyle was intuitive enough to realize as long as I attempted to do as instructed, I was given credit.

At that point, Ms. Guilfoyle encouraged my parents to have me start school at Boettcher School. This school was right across the street from Children's Hospital at 19th and Downing. At the time, it was part of the Denver Public School system and it served the needs of physical and mental disabled children. I remember establishing some great friendships there with people who were just as intelligent. The first person who comes to mind is Joe Lujan. Joe has cerebral palsy, however, he was able to walk and much more mobile than I was. Joe was always walking around with an unbalanced gate, and yet he was still able to keep his balance. Joe was also very smart, who had a very strong demeanor and zest for life. As we got older, Joe took the job at Fitzsimmons Hospital in their athletic department. I believe eventually he became the Director of Athletics, and then was transferred to a branch hospital in Colorado Springs, Colorado, where I believe he had the same position and eventually received a promotion. He worked there for close to 30 years and just recently retired. He truly exemplified the definition of personal perseverance.

I attended Boettcher School until my junior year in high school. I believe I was scholastically challenged up until the 9th or 10th grade when I realized that the school was more geared toward vocational development/placement rather than educational development. Consequently, in my junior year, my mother, Shirlee Mueller, started investigating the possibility of me attending a regular high school in a scholastically challenging environment. I believe my mother also knew my spirit and knew the best place for me to flourish would be in a Christian high school environment. The first school my mother contacted was Machebeuf High School. This was a Catholic school, which was more than willing to accept me as a student. The second school my mother contacted was Denver Lutheran High School.

I can remember visualizing my mother talking to the high school counselor, Ed Mertz, who was more than willing to meet me and discuss the possibility of attending school there. However, the Principal at the time, Mr. Norman Brinkman, was very reluctant in the phone conversation and suggested that I attend the Cerebral Palsy Center for vocational development. My mother was very adamant in expressing that he was missing the point, and asked again if we could meet them the following day. I can also remember the high school counselor, Ed Mertz, being very excited to meet the both of us. Let me tell you right now, that my Lord Jesus Christ does amazing miracles. When I arrived at the high school, the whole school was on one floor. As we went into Mr. Mertz office, Mr. Brinkman was there and he had a total change of heart overnight. They both were more than willing to accept me and to give me an opportunity. What a miracle! I can also remember going back to Boettcher School and telling them of my plans and my parents being told that I could not handle it academically or socially in a regular high school setting.

Consequently, I was required to take another IQ test. Upon completion, the psychologist who administered the test told the special ed school that while I was not a genius [we all know that], I was not stupid either and should be given the opportunity. So here is another part of the miracle. In order to not be totally overwhelmed by everything, my parents along with Ed Mertz came up with the idea of me attending Boettcher School in the morning and having a Denver Public School bus take me to the private school in the afternoon. Another miracle! My junior year I took German I and Business Law. So, in other words, the message was sink or swim. After my first semester there, I had a 3.5 average. That Spring, I went back to the special ed school and politely showed them my GPA, with the message being I'm out of here. I ended up enrolling full time to Denver Lutheran High School my senior year, and graduated with a 3.3 average. Of course, I had good times too. More specifically, I became actively involved in drama, and the teacher, a Mr. Dino Pochelli, took interest in me, and I knew he was in my corner and really believed in me.

He even made me a character in the Brer Rabbit stories. I did the voice and somebody else did the muppet.

There is another story that I believe needs to be shared. First, I need to explain to you that I am a very social being with numerous friendships. Most of them are like family. Anyway, my senior year I wanted to go to prom, and I had my eye on somebody. Her name was Jeanie Woods. A friend of mine, a Mr. Brandt Domas, offered to be my chauffeur for the evening. My mother, knowing how expensive it would be to take her out to dinner, offered to make a steak dinner and leave the whole house for the three of us. Upon picking her up and bringing her back to the house, both of my parents were gone and nowhere to be found. I walked into the family room and my mother already had a table setting set out with a candle-lit dinner and steaks ready to go. What a wonderful mother! At this point, you need a job to know that I'm unable to feed myself. So, Brandt leaned over and whispered in my ear, "Do you want me to feed you, or do you want her to?" My response was, "I don't care." Well, he ended up feeding me. We then proceeded to go to a dance in Lakewood, and Brandt ended up staying in my 1973 Dodge Sportsman van, listening to music while Jeanie and I were at the dance. At the end of the dance, Brandt whispered in my ear, "If you need help, just send somebody out to get me. "What a great friend! After the dance was over, Brandt again whispered in my ear, "You need to take her out for dessert." I asked him where we should go, and he said, "The Magic Pan where they serve crepes." We get to the restaurant, and he again whispers in my ear, "Who do you want to feed you?" This time I knew Jeanie heard me say, "I don't care." As it turned out, they both ended up feeding me. Upon taking her home, Brandt parked the car, cleared his voice and stepped out of the car, and stood behind the van smoking a cigarette, figuring we were going to have a make out session or something.

At this juncture, I want to talk about surrounding yourself with people who truly believe in you. This is a form of restoration. Restoration of the individual and the people around him. I'm going to use Scripture to exemplify this point. The Bible verse that I have decided to use is 2 Corinthians 4:5 –6 which says in the New International Version: For what is preached is not for ourselves but Jesus Christ as Lord, as ourselves your servants for Jesus' sake. For God who said "Let light shine out of darkness, make His light shine in our hearts to give us the light of the knowledge of God displayed in the face of Christ." That being said, the people mentioned above have been or continue to be examples of this as it is stated in Scripture. I must also make the point that my parents lived every day like this and wore Jesus' sandals every day.

Going back, one thing I remember is going to Children's Hospital for physical therapy 2-3 times a week. One memory I have is when I was 11 -12 years old, my brother's baseball coach, George Prowse, who was a real mentor for my brother Todd and a local member of the Optimist Club Service Organization bought me an adult size three-wheel bicycle. I would ride that around the neighborhood almost every day. It was great physical exercise for me. Once in a while, my mother could not find me because I could be as far as six blocks away. I also can remember my mother having a distinct mouth whistle for my two brothers to come home for dinner. It could be heard from miles away. I think my mother also had a whistle for me to come home although she did not use it that much being that I was already home or with them anyway. When I got the bike, I think my mother forgot the whistle she made for me therefore she had to go looking for me.

At this point, there is something very personal that I believe needs to be shared. First, I want to share with you that growing up and realizing that I had a disability was not easy. I had many questions as to why God had chosen me to have a disability. Yes, there were times when I was very upset, angry and confused. These questions lingered for a long period of time as time went on. A lot of time, I would try not to think about it and just try to move on. During my formative years, my mother and I had some very heart-warming moments. My mother would take time every day to kind of "check in" to see how I was doing. It was during those times when I would share my frustrations and questions. My mother in turn provided great insight on different situations. During this time in my life, I would often ask God or whomever "Why me, why not somebody else?" There were times when I felt depressed and no way out of the situation. I remember thinking "Why is my life situation different and no one really understands the struggles or the circumstances which I was left to deal with every day. I would share these thoughts and feelings with my mother and I know she understood where I was coming from. I'm sure that both of my parents prayed for me, however with God's help, I was the one who needed to figure it out.

CHAPTER II

My Upbringing

Growing up, both of my brothers were very scholastically and athletically inclined. They were both very good at basketball and baseball. We were a very close-knit family and very supportive of one another. Despite this, my mother knew that I had some unique challenges that I needed help figuring out. One thing that my mother used to tell me was that despite how successful my brothers may be in the future; I was still considered the oldest brother. For this reason, they would always look up to me as a guidepost of how to live and handle life. That has stuck with me to this day. In Scripture, the weight of a mother's heart for her children is written in Proverbs 31:25-29 saying, "25 She is clothed with strength and dignity; she can laugh at the days to come. 26 She speaks with wisdom, and faithful instruction is on her tongue. 27 She watches over the affairs of her household and does not eat the bread of idleness. 28 Her children arise and call her blessed; her husband also, and he praises her: 29 Many women do noble things, but you surpass them all."

My father taught me how to be strong. An example of this occurred to me when he would say, "Never feel sorry for yourself. For there is always someone else who is going through more than you, and count your blessings." On the lighter side, my father always had a joyful heart. Having a joyful heart, even though he suffered with rheumatoid arthritis continuously, you would actually never know how much he suffered. A memory I have related to my father is when I was 16 years old. As a kid, every summer I would go to Easter Seal Handicamp for two weeks at a time. About this time, I became really interested in women around my age or older. There was a camp counselor by the name of Delaine Hogan who caught my eye. Anyway, as the story goes, she was living in Denver at the time and I really wanted to take her out. In conversations with her over the phone, I found out where she lived. Very sly don't you think? It was a Saturday afternoon and I convinced my father to take me by her apartment. When we arrived, she was not there. What I remember is my father driving around the city of Denver for several hours, waiting for her to come home. Once she finally got home, my father knocked on the door. She opened the door, and my father subtly walked away so I could have some privacy. I ended up asking her out and surprisingly she agreed. I was so excited! My first actual date. I cannot remember what we did, but it was a great time and I was nervous periodically as all get out. As a reference point for Scripture, Proverbs 22:6 says, "Train up a child in the way he should go; even when he is old he will not depart from it." In addition, 1 Thessalonians 2:11-12 says, "For you know that we dealt with each of you as a father deals with his own children, encouraging, comforting and urging you to live lives worthy of God, who calls you into his kingdom and glory." Reflecting on my father, who passed away in November 2020, this is exactly how he lived. While being stern when he needed to be, my father exemplified how to carry the Cross of Christ and placing his feet in Jesus' sandals every day.

CHAPTER III

Crossroads

When reflecting on what my parents accomplished with their children, it's absolutely amazing. God willing, in writing this book, I believe that it is important to find, identify and walk in your own personal way with our Lord and Savior Jesus Christ. It is important to note that God can handle anything we throw at him. Some of these include anger, frustration and questions as we walk through this temporary life. At this point, I want to take the opportunity to show that God can handle all of our emotions. More recently, I have had friends share with me the loss of loved ones, like their own child. For example, my friend, Wendy, lost her daughter when she was 18 years old. In talking to Wendy later, she told me that she was very angry at God for taking her child. She knew intrinsically that God could handle and accept any and all emotions she was feeling. Years later, Wendy knows that her daughter is in heaven laughing, playing and requesting that God protects the family.

My other friends, Jon and Monique, lost their daughter in an automobile accident near I-25 in 2017. While Jon and Monique have dealt with the loss of their daughter, even with God's help, it is still difficult for them. They continue to give themselves to others, including myself with a joyful and giving heart. Jon has told me that he talks to Mary Sue every day, which provides solace for his heart. I can't imagine what they must be experiencing. I think about their daughter, Sadie, who is the rock of the family. Her siblings see this in her every day. God has blessed her with a son, Benson's and I have seen the joy in his eyes, which Nathan and Sadie Henry have provided. On November ---- - 2022, their second son was born Keller Henry. May God continue to bless you and your family.

In looking back, there were other individuals that have impacted my life. The next vignette is about a man who is carefree, fun loving and charismatic. His name is Roger Davis who I met in the Summer of 1978. He was assigned as my camp counselor at a summer camp for the physically and mentally challenged. He always had a way of making people laugh. Roger was in Graduate School at UNC studying Special-Education. I was just entering my Sophomore Year and we totally connected. I can remember going to his house in Greeley, Colorado on a Friday or Saturday night and making Strawberry, Banana and Peach Daiquiris. On more than one occasion, we would go to a restaurant in town and he would manually push my chair into the Women's Restroom and leave me sitting in there until someone would come in and take me back to our table. On another occasion, we went to this drinking establishment called Paul's Place, which was a biker bar and a fight broke out. My date and I were only 18 years old at the time and the bartender, Roger, and another friend of ours Richard Nelligan helped carry me outside up a flight of stairs just as the police arrived at the scene. What a close call! To this day we have remained friends and he has a wonderful wife named Renée. Roger and René are totally committed to their Lord and Savior Christ Jesus and have their offspring Cossette, Lavanna, Tavi and their families committed to Christ Jesus. When Roger and Renée first met, they began going on missionary trips to Third World countries to show God's love for them and teaching The Gospel. Roger has always had a heart for people which shines through every day. Just recently, Roger was diagnosed with Multiple Sclerosis, and yet continues to give of himself to this population, by joining and establishing support groups. Again, another example of wearing Jesus' sandals. Roger, you are also a great example to me as to how to be a great leader and yet have a carefree spirit. Thank you!

I have just recently [for several years now] had a friend who was diagnosed with Ovarian Cancer. A year ago, she went into remission. However, that darn old cancer came back again. She was in Hospice and passed away in April 2022. I must be honest with you. I tasseled with God regarding Roshaun's medical condition repeatedly, and it has even got to the point where I have angrily asked God why He has taken such a beautiful woman away from her teenage kids and husband. In private conversations with God, I know that He has been able to handle all my questions. In turn, He has provided to me a peace that when He takes her into His heavenly kingdom, it will be a joyous day. My prayer is that the same calmness and reassurance will reside in each family heart. I have realized that this might take some time, however, everything is in God's hands. These are the Scriptures that I believe provide God's sovereign direction: Hebrews 5:7 says, "During the days of Jesus' life on earth, he offered up prayers and petitions with fervent cries and tears to the one who could save him from death, and he was heard because of his reverent submission." In addition, Psalm 34:15 says, "The eyes of the Lord are toward the righteous and his ears toward their cry." Lastly, Zechariah 1:17 says, "Proclaim further: This is what the Lord Almighty says: 'My towns will again overflow with prosperity, and the Lord will again comfort Zion and choose Jerusalem.'"

My life changed drastically when I was 14-15 years old. As I have mentioned before, my friend Brandt Domas who was 17-18 at the time. Brandt intuitively made a conscious effort to take me under his wings. Brandt over time began to show me how to be spiritually strong and yet be free at the same time. Additionally, the Adult Youth Leaders at the time were Dale and Melinda Peterson. Dale also was very impactful in my life as to how to be spiritually free and have fun [laughing, joking etc.] at the same time. I can remember that on one occasion we all went to Kansas City, Missouri for a youth retreat. We took a charter bus to our destination. There were several other churches who were on the trip. Anyway, Dale volunteered to take care of me during the retreat. Brandt and another friend Mark Olson also volunteered to take care of me. All I can remember was laughing continuously for the next four days. At that point, I realized they all had something special. One day, I went with them to hear a pastor preach about the Gospel. At that point, I can remember sitting in the back of one of the ballrooms and Jesus tapping on my shoulder and my heart telling me if I would surrender my life to Him, we could do this journey together. At that point, I surrendered my life to Jesus and He has guided me in each way. It was then that I began to accept myself and the disability I was given. I truly, truly believe that God has anointed my life and His angels are watching and interceding for me each day. I also know that I am a sinner and that I must ask for forgiveness, grace and mercy every day.

As I have previously mentioned, there are times when God tells us when to stand on and to stand up for what we believe in the while knowing that our God is right beside us. There are however other times when God calls us to be still. As I get older, the more I realize that this is true. Letting God take over is of utmost importance, and letting Him handle life's situations. My remaining silent is sometimes more powerful than the spoken word. Throughout my whole life, God has always had a special eye on me to ensure that I will always be protected because I am very special in His eyes. My responsibility in return is to radiate the love of Christ. As a result, I then trust that I am right in the palm of God's hand and can demonstrate poise, assurance and His loving authority in my life. I look at the special bonds, specifically friendships that have been graciously showered upon me only by His grace. These friendships are very near and dear to my heart. Most of them are like family for which I am truly grateful. For I know through any situation we are there for each other. The purpose and reason for my blessed life is to show a happy carefree Christ-like lifestyle and to not take life so seriously. Yes, life does have challenges along the way, however, does not take away the gift the life every day. For we must live every day to the fullest, that our life is a gift, that every day in the gift with new opportunities. We have a choice to either rejoice or totally neglect when God has provided for us. Consequently, I try to look at what does God want me to do today, more specifically what does He want me to accomplish today. Let me give you some examples of how this has been orchestrated in my own life. Since I don't have the ability to use my arms or legs to do certain tasks, I've had to use my cognitive skills to compensate for my physical abilities. Because of this, I have graciously been given the ability to listen intently to what is happening in someone's life and provide some insight. Another important aspect is to be nonjudgmental as people share their joys and struggles. In this process, you need to place your own agenda aside while still providing insight on the potential outcomes of their decision.

The next phase of my life is to express and to experience feeling honest joy. This has happened throughout my life. First, there are so many ways to experience joy. You must have a joyful heart. People who see me and get to know me know that I am a real thrill seeker. The first thing I do is I really don't think of myself as being any different from anybody else. My wheelchair is just an extension of myself to get from one point to another. While there are times when life sends you friendly reminders, this is not a focal point of who I am. I have experienced so many opportunities in life to where people are totally astonished by those mastering experiences. These include downhill snow skiing at Winter Park, being up in a hot air balloon, hang gliding in an airplane, flying out of State of Colorado on my own. Let me expand on this more. Looking back on my childhood experiences, going to a camp for special needs children, adolescents and adults was very special. At this camp, you were given the opportunity to do "normal" childhood stuff. The activities included horseback riding, riflery, archery, fishing and swimming. I can remember having a sense of freedom and learning how to love myself. This is where I began to accept myself and my disability of cerebral palsy. This was also a place where I really began to love myself, others, as well as experience freedom and true joy. Even though the goal of this autobiography is to embrace and understand God's grace and understanding of each and every one of us, I feel like it is important to share my wild side. Earlier in this book, I mentioned my good friend Roger Davis. Well, this next story also involved him. One night after taking a shower and getting ready for bed, he asked me if I wanted to go streaking. Of course without hesitation I agreed to do so. Several things happen that night that was just hilarious! The funny thing is I was I stark naked with Roger pushing my wheelchair. Roger of course was too chicken to go stark naked and wore a pair of gym shorts. Secondly, one of the counselor's named Alisha, as we were running past her cabin asked us to stop so she could take a picture. You also need to know I was the first and only streaker of the camp. I can remember the Camp Director Dave Holstein telling my summer counselor Roger, that if it was anybody else but Tracy, he would have been fired. I know there is no way they would get away with that today. But for me, it was just part of the growing up process, and I would take none of that away. At this point, I want to express my tremendous gratitude towards my mother and father for allowing me to experience life so wonderfully.

In September 1977, I started attending the University of Northern Colorado. The Director of Disabled Services was Teddy Scharff. She was also disabled and confined to a power wheelchair. In getting to know Mrs. Scharff, she initially gave the impression that I would be living in a dorm setting and someone would always be there to take care of my personal needs. As it turned out upon my arrival on September 19, 1977 the dormitory, Harrison Hall room 115, I was told that certain people would come in and take care of me during certain hours of the day. More specifically, to get me up in the morning and put me to bed in the evening. Fortunately, I had an old friend of mine by the name of Bill Eberhardt who was also a student, and he took me under his wing. We would get together for lunch and dinner until I was able to build a substantial group of friendships. As you know, this did not take a long time. I'm very shy. Not! It was probably the best thing that happened to me. I can remember my father standing there in the doorway of my dorm room, and he had to just walk away. He just wasn't sure how it was going to work out. My mother stayed with my cousin, Dave Gerhke, and his wife, LaVonne, that first evening. My mother came by my dorm room at 8:30 the next morning, and I was already up and about, having breakfast. I think at that point, she knew I was going to be okay. Initially, there were two people taking care me. Later, Mrs. Scharff assisted in getting lined up with a home health care agency called Northeast Home Healthcare. There was one person that I can remember that took care of me for many, many years. Her name was Noreen Dreher. She was probably in her 50s or 60s at the time and she became like my second mom. I can remember telling her almost anything from relationships, girlfriend problems, or school to whatever. She probably knew more about my girlfriend problems than my own mother. That was okay, because she was a very wise woman with a ton of wisdom. What I find interesting is God has sprinkled what I truly believe are angels throughout my life. May I profess that it is still true to this day.

God continued to sprinkle me with the utmost crazy angels during this time in my life. During my Freshman Year, God was able to hook me up with a group called UNC Christian Fellowship Group. There were three main leaders of the group, Jon Boreland, Dennis Veilleux and Jim Kadlacheck. They were all pretty laid back, however, they were both committed in their walk with Christ. At that time, I started attending First United Presbyterian Church. A number of people from UNC Fellowship also attended Sunday services. The pastor was Jim Farley and he was able to uniquely take Scripture and apply it to everyday living. He also had a great sense of humor which kept me locked in every Sunday morning. I was also blessed with meeting some wonderful people who I connected with which included Rowland "Butch" and Sandee Strobel, Tad and Jane Gilmore, Rob and Marikay Cassaday, along with many other people. To this day, they are still devout

Christians and continue to be an example to follow. They have taught me how to walk humbly and how to serve others and mirror Christ.

While attending the University of Northern Colorado I had some great times. One of my fondest memories was going to a restaurant called, The Junction, which was two blocks from the dorm. We would walk down there anywhere between 10:30 and 12:00 midnight several times a month for M&M cookies. They were the greatest! However, there is another side of the story that I want to share. On more than one occasion, I would go to the restaurant, specifically with Mike, Bob, Brian, Steve, and after we had eaten, they would see a group of UNC women sitting at a table, probably catty-corner from us, and one of those three of them would turn my manual wheelchair around, purposefully unlock my brakes and put their foot on the back of my chair and push me just enough until I would roll up the ladies' table. On other occasions, we would go to the movie theater and before the movie would start, they would move me to the front of the movie theater and turn me to face the audience while they went back to their seats. As this kept occurring, I eventually came up with the idea of telling the audience that we were from the Juvenile Detention Center and we had them on a reacclimation project. Talk about embarrassing, they rarely did that again.

At this juncture, I must tell you about my good friend Mike Finnefrock. Mike, who is a very devout Christian was also very actively involved with UNC Christian Fellowship. When I first met Mike in 1979, he was very flamboyant, energetic, spontaneous, and funny. At dinnertime we would meet up in the dorm and at times there were 15-20 people, where we were all friends having dinner together. There were other times where Mike and I would sit in the dining area for hours and just talk or wait for people just to sit with us. There were other times when I would be sound asleep and Mike would come in 2 or 3 AM and talk about whatever. As time went on, I began to meet some wonderful people, like Brian DeHerrea, Robyn Rundle, Glen Graff, James Smallwood, Laurie Lee, and many others. I remember, I think it was my Junior Year at UNC, there were six women living in a house and they use to invite us all for dinner at least once a week. What a great memory. Of course, they were all wonderful and they spoiled every one of the guys. Myself included! Of their group, there were several that I was interested in dating, however, I never asked them out because I did not want to mess up what we already had. There were several women in the house that I could tell them anything and be comfortable. The same could be said for both Mike and Bob. They were both fun to hang out with and absolutely hilarious. This is even true today. Yet, they both have a very serious side with great perspective and insight. To this day, I can still share my deepest thoughts.

Looking back, I think it was also my Junior Year and we compiled an intramural football and basketball team called the "Kids of The King." A friend of mine, Jim Nall who was also quadriplegic where the Honorary Head Coaches and we had some very competitive, very athletic players. For football I think we came in second place out of 16 teams. For basketball we won the whole thing. Our goal was to be competitive while still honoring our Lord and Savior Jesus Christ. I can remember my parents driving up from Denver play. Another great memory I will never forget!

I remember on one occasion where Mike and another friend went to Boulder Reservoir to go water skiing. The whole time I was just planning on sitting in the boat and in enjoying the Summertime whether. Well, Mike and Chris Fuller had totally different ideas. They told me they thought I should have the experience of water skiing. You need to know that I had tried this at Lake Powell in Utah with Bob Rue and a group of friends several years earlier [as I recall Mike and Chris were also there] and it was not a fun experience. Anyway, they put me in the water against my will and Chris would cradle my body in his arms sideways and hang on to the rope behind the boat at the same time.

Michael was driving the boat and he was not driving at a high rate of speed so the water overcame my whole body and I felt like I was going to drown. I can remember having my hand in the air trying to signal to him to let go of the rope. I think he realized that once he did not see my face, he needed to let go. Thank God! I do know that all their intentions were good and they just wanted me to experience what they were experiencing.

On another occasion my friends asked to borrow my 1973 Dodge Van to go on a double date. I remember they had asked me to go with them, and I originally told them that I was not going to go and that I did not want to be a third wheel. However, they continue to be very persistent and I reluctantly agreed to go. This happened in mid-November, so it was extremely cold and snowy. On the way home, the van ran out of gas. So, Brian and Mike ended up leaving to get some gasoline, while leaving us behind. Later, they told me that I had planned it that way. I did not however as the story goes, it worked out for my benefit. I believe these stories exemplifies how God wants us to live, to experience all the joys of life. More specifically, to be again carefree and laugh out loud wholeheartedly with a smile on your beautiful face. I know we all have had the life experience of being around either an individual or a group of people where they bring so much joy that there is a constant smile on your face. I have experienced this more times than I can count. Consequently, I try to surround myself with this type of demeanor as much as possible. I have also noticed the carefree Christ-like persona that they carried which is so attractive. Herein lies the answer to everything your heart desires: Totally surrendering everything we have to experience the joy He so openly wants to give to us.

In the Summer of 1982, the Denver Broncos started having their training camp at the University of Northern Colorado. I can remember training camp had just started at Butler Hancock Field right across from the parking lot of my dormitory. I decided to make a jaunt over to the practice field just to get a glimpse of what was happening. As practice was ending, I see newly hired coach Dan Reeves coming towards me in a golf cart. He stops and we started talking. I can remember him saying to me specifically "Hi, I'm Dan Reeves." I kind of chuckled inside and introduced myself. The thing he did not know was I used to watch him as a kid when he played for the Dallas Cowboys. His jersey number was 30 and he was the fullback and would block for Walt Garrison. He later became an assistant coach under Tom Landry. So, I knew more about him than he thought. Anyway, as we were talking, he tells Dan Bill, the head equipment manager, to go and get me a press pass. Every year after that I would get a press pass. Some other memories include meeting assistant coaches Charlie West and Merle Moore. During practice, the first place I would head for was where the linebackers were practicing and Merle Moore was the positions coach. I would love watching him teach and train how to use your footwork for that position. Whenever I arrived, he always acknowledged that I was there. He would also take time after practice just to talk. It never really was about football, it was about family and friends, the people we were close to. As a result, we became extremely close and very good friends. During the season, I would also call Dan Reeves periodically from work and just talk. Most of the time, we would talk about both of our families, and he would specifically talk about his grandchildren. On one occasion, I was able to meet his father Ed Reeves and boy, that was an honor. One last story that I would like to you. First, I need to tell you that my parents used to have an employment service called ACIM Personnel Service. Anyway, one day in the Spring of 1988 get a call from my mother and she tell me that she is organizing a father-son banquet at Cross of Glory Lutheran Church, the church I grew up in. She goes on to ask me if I could get either Assistant Coach Mike Shanahan or Merle Moore to speak at the banquet. I knew both and they were great Christian men. At the time, I told my mother that I probably could get Dan Reeves to speak, who also was a follower of Jesus. Of course, my mother did not think this was possible, however I told her that I would talk to him. Several days later, I called Dan with my request. He told me he would be honored to be a guest speaker, so I gave him the phone number. He then proceeded to call my mother at work, which I know astonished her. I think my father was also surprised. Anyway, she gave him the date and he showed up. I remember my mother organizing a buffet type breakfast which everyone participated in. I remember sitting catty corner from Dan at the breakfast, my father feeding me and my heart filled with so much joy. Dan did a great job of sharing his testimony. All these stories are some of my fondest memories.

As far as school was concerned, I would get people who were on the Work Study Program, and they would help take notes for me. They would also help me with homework or study time. When this service was not available, I would see if anyone there I knew and if they were, I would slide a piece of carbon paper under their notes. If not, I would scan the room for meticulous note taker and ask them if I could just slide a piece of carbon paper underneath their notes. It was a great way to get to know people. Almost everyone that I had the pleasure of getting to know were fun, energetic and great just to hang out. I would also occasionally ask them out for dinner, movie or just to do something together. Let's just say, I knew how and still do enjoy my life and live it to the fullest. To this day, I remain in touch and maintain those relationships. I am so blessed!

Chapter IV

Life Is Full of Journeys Along the Way

Previously I had mentioned my friend Bob. To this day our friendship has remained extremely strong. Bob is a true brother to me. He is a kind and gentle man who knows his source and purpose is for our Lord and Savior Jesus Christ. We met each other in the Fall of 1978. Bob tells a story of us first meeting each other when he was 16 years old. More specifically, Bob told me that we met at a Christian Fellowship called The Barn where I gave my personal testimony. Bob has this amazing personality and sense of humor. He could be in the room, make a simple comment and make everybody start laughing. To this day, we may not see each other for 6-8 months and yet we are able to pick up right where we left off. In between times, we still talk to each other on the phone and he still knows how to make me laugh. What a great friend and what a great blessing. He is truly like a brother to me, someone who I trust implicitly. Upon graduation, Bob was hired as a PE teacher at Columbine Elementary in Longmont, Colorado. He taught there for the next 30 years. A characteristic which I appreciate the most is that he is nonjudgmental. While you know where he firmly stands, Bob is a tremendous listener and offers his wisdom when it is necessary. His wife, Lisa is a wonderful Godly woman and a tremendous servant for Christ. She was the Founder of Friends First, a nonprofit business that promotes teen sexual abstinence, the dangers within, the importance of remaining abstinence and to keep this within the sanctity of marriage. The last several years, they have been serving at a Church Retreat Camp in Marble, Colorado specifically for pastors who may be experiencing burnout. What a great calling.

Bob and Lisa were married on June 22, 1986 and I was truly honored to be one of Bob's groomsmen. Their family grew quickly and they had Sarah and Rick. From the beginning they knew me as Uncle Tracy. To this day, they still address me in the same way. They are in their adulthood now and I am extremely proud. Rick is an apprentice working with different kinds of metal. I know he has built a wine holding cabinet for his parents and he is now working for his brother-in-law making different kinds of fabrications. Additionally, he just bought a house in Johnstown, Colorado near his sister and brother-in-law. Lawrence and Sarah Nee. They have three wonderful children, Rylan, Owen and Gavin. They are both great parents and have provided a loving, joyful, playful and safe home with Christ at the center of their foundation.

To make the story more intriguing is that I met Bob's sister Robyn when she was 11 years old. I remember going to his parents' residence and Bob making barbecued spare ribs on the grill. They were the best in the world! I also remember a time when Bob introduced me to downhill skiing at Winter Park, Colorado. He told me that they had a handicap ski program there and we should go check it out. I reluctantly agreed to do so. Anyway, the first time we went up occurred when the program was still in the infant stages. As I recall, we were also with another friend of Bob's, Steve Seltloffer, who was dating his other sister Rhonda at the time. I had an instructor who was very well trained. Her responsibility was to help tether the sled from behind, helping me to make left and right turns. The apparatus I sat in was like a toboggan like sled with ski rudders underneath. Anyway, after making some practice skill runs on some designated green and blue slopes for beginners, Bob asked if he could give it a try on the tether. As it went, I noticed that we were going down the hill at a high rate of speed and all of a sudden, I hear the instructor shout "Look out, you're going down a Black Diamond." Now, I knew I was the only a beginner and I also knew that Black Diamond meant only one thing and that we were on an expert slope. So, we eventually were able to stop and survey the area. We were told by the instructor that on the other side of the trees there was a Blue Slope on the other side. So, as it went, we ended up treading through a set of trees where the snow was at least thigh-high. At one point, they lost me and I ended up face down in the snow. After going through the trees, I felt the toboggan start to take off down the hill towards another set of trees. I looked behind and nobody grabbed the tether. Bob and Steve were skiing beside me trying to catch and Steve ended up getting in front page of and laying his body down to stop the sled. Fortunately, nobody ended up hurting themselves and we all had a good laugh.

More about Bob's sister Robyn. Robyn ended up attending Colorado State University and marrying her high school sweetheart Pat Brady who also attended CSU. I did not actually meet Pat until 1990 at their wedding. As time went on Pat, Robyn and myself became closer and our friendship grew from there. Again, I believe it was another divine intervention from God. Thinking about this further, my father used to say that if you look at it, God's divine intervention happens every day. It is so true! So, when Robyn and Pat had their first child, Kelsey, I went to Poudre Valley Hospital the next day and held Kelsey for the first time. Later, I was told that I was the first one to hold her. From that point forward I was known as Uncle Tracy. They subsequently had three more children, paternal twins Keegan, Tucker [1998] and Maggie [2001]. As I was there at the hospital the next day to welcome them into the world. The part that is the most meaningful in that they had asked me to be a godparent to their newborn son, Tucker. What an honor and a privilege. I remember when Tucker was first born, we were at a family gathering and Robyn was unable to stop Tucker from crying. I asked Robyn if I could hold him. As it happens, he quit crying right away. I know this might embarrass him, however, it is still there in my memory bank and will be something I will never forget. I knew then that through God's divine intervention we were meant to be together. They have all since grown up and leading their own lives. Despite this, I remain close with all of them, especially Tucker and Kelsey, who check in with me on a consistent basis. As they both have grown into adulthood our relationship has changed and we talk about joyful happenings or concerns of the heart. What a blessing it is to have this family in my life.

Chapter V: Handling Life's Challenges Head on with Grace and Mercy

In this Chapter, I want to take the opportunity to discuss how God has anointed my life by giving me the courage to stand up, listen and guide my footsteps along the way. To start I must say it has taken a lot of perseverance and personal fortitude to accomplish what I have achieved thus far in my life. Let me start off this way. This is where my faith is so important. I want to start out with some Scripture, specifically Philippians 4:13, when Apostle Paul wrote from prison to the Philippians "I can do all things through Christ who strengthens me." Before I continue, this was also the laid upon my heart. In your own life, what is holding you in prison in your own personal life? For those who feel they are being held in prison whether it be emotional, psychological, physical, financial or whatever, remember to hand it over and to address the situation together while listening to God. So many times, we believe we know what is best without praying or talking to God first. More specifically, pray for His direction and I personally believe that He will give to you His thoughts for a specific decision we need to make. Remember, God's time frame is quite different, therefore we need to wait quietly for God's answer. Remember, this is God's answer, not ours and that He loves all of us. Even though there are times [more often than not) when I think everything is under control when it is not. It is then when I turn directly to God with the intersession of the Holy Spirit and I ask God for direction, guidance and peace. While talking to the Lord, I make sure that I back up and thank Him for all the blessings he has already given to me. Also, if I listen intently, God will provide the right people at the right time to discuss the situation. The direction I receive does not happen until down the road when He speaks to me. Usually this happens to me in the morning when I am getting dressed and ready for the day. I can remember my mother telling me to prioritize and to get the hard stuff done in the morning when I am mentally sharp. I believe this is true in my own spiritual life. It is funny that He talks to me usually in the bathroom while I'm washing my hair or shaving. He may also wake me up in the middle of the night to talk to me or just give me a thought. What a great sense of humor He has!

In talking about my work experience, I definitely did not take the normal path. As an Undergraduate I worked as a volunteer on two crisis intervention hotlines. The first hotline was called Weld Information and Referral Services. The second was called In Touch Hotline Services. The Volunteer Director for In Touch Hotline services was Debbie Beck who was also a student at UNC. We became extremely close and she became one of my best friends. She knew with me that she could trust me with anything and she knew after training me I could handle anything on the crisis intervention hotline. I did this for about one year and there were times when we would work together and be up until 2 AM. When a crisis call would come in we would coach each other how to handle a situation. This could be from a potential drug overdose or a potential suicide call. There were times when I would be on the phone trying to talk or calm the person down and trying to find their address or where they were located. Debbie or whomever I was working with would be on the other phoneline either calling the Greeley Police Department or the Northern Colorado Medical Center for an ambulance. I believe this was just the start how God strategically placed me to uniquely reach out to people in need. The storyline continued in 1982 when I worked as an intern at Greeley West High School. I can remember when I first inquired about doing my internship at the high school, the Director of the Counseling Center's name was Marcia Osborne. As we began to discuss the possibilities, she recognized the need for helping troubled adolescents who were on academic probation. She also believed I thought that I would be a good fit as a good listener and role model. As time went on, we both began sharing our Christian faith with each other. Again, another example of divine intervention. While there, I ended up working with adolescents who had some issues around self-esteem, social, academic and other struggles. Some, I'm sure had drug or alcohol problem at the time. Looking back, it was amazing how after a period of time the adolescents who were struggling began to feel comfortable and just started to open up. I thoroughly enjoyed working at the high school.

In the Winter/Spring of 1984, I was working on my Master's Degree and I worked as an intern at an outpatient drug and alcohol facility called The Institute for Alcohol Awareness. More specifically, the purpose was to provide education and treatment for Court Ordered DUI offenders. For the first 4-6 months, I would observe the Director Mark Wendoff how he would run the groups. He also had another employee, Bill "Choppy " Herron who also ran the education/therapy groups. They were both Certified Addiction Counselors [CAC III] what was known as the Alcohol and Drug Abuse Division [ADAD], which was under the Department of Health for the State of Colorado. While interning I was also receiving hours which would go towards my own certification. For the first 4-6 months, I learned from them how to run a group. After a period, I began co-facilitating the groups primarily with Mr. Wendoff. Upon completion of my internship and obtaining my Master's Degree in Rehabilitation Counseling, I inquired about becoming a part-time employee. I was hired in March 1984 and continued co-facilitating groups as well as running groups on my own. At this juncture, it is important for you, the reader, to understand how the Judicial System works in the State of Colorado. When someone is arrested for a DUI [Driving Under the Influence] or a DWAI [Driving While Ability Impaired], they go through the Judicial System and appear in Court. After about 6 to 9 months of hearings/plea bargains/proceedings the defendant is placed on probation usually for 12-18 months. After this occurs, they are required to be seen by an Alcohol/Drug Evaluation Specialist [Probation Officer] for the presiding district. Once the evaluation is completed, they are sent to a licensed facility specifically for this type of offender. Of course, there is more criteria the Probation Officer must take into account, however for you, the reader, that is enough minutia for you to know. Ha, ha, did I just say that?

Over time, I learned how to facilitate groups and create a safe comfortable environment. Again, this is what I was called to do. Occasionally, a client would come in early just to talk casually or to tell me what was going on in their life, whether it be positive or troublesome. These situations confirmed what I was called to do.

In May 1992, I was told by the Director that he needed to scale back his business overhead and needed to let me go. Initially, I was very upset because I had dedicated my last 8.5 years of my life. This anger was short-lived however and God told me that he had much bigger plans. While the situation and circumstances were still on the hot plate, I asked my former employer to write me a letter of recommendation. I also had the people who I have worked for in the past write letters of recommendation.

At that time, I knew how the Colorado Judicial System worked, especially for DUI and DWAI offenders. Consequently, my thought process changed and I decided that I wanted to be a probation officer for the State of Colorado. At the same time, the federal government under the George Bush Sr. Administration passed the Americans with Disabilities Act. As I'm sure you are aware, if an employer were to hire someone with a disability "reasonable accommodations" were now required by law. Over the next six months, I had approximately 20-25 interviews from El Paso County [Colorado Springs], Arapahoe County [South of Denver], Denver County, Adams County [Brighton], Weld County [Greeley and surrounding areas] and Larimer County. I seriously had friends who would drive my van to all the interviews. In the interview process, I would take the approach of totally selling myself out. By this, I mean I had to take the initiative of telling them how I would handle certain and sometimes difficult situations despite my physical disability. I knew intrinsically they legally could not ask me any of these questions, however, I knew my role was to be honest and to eliminate any kind of doubt which the interviewers may have. My goal was to educate them, along with all the while focused on my strengths on what I could provide to them. While I had this mindset on every interview, I knew intrinsically that I was my responsibility to educate them on my strengths and adaptability. At this point, I want to tell you about my very last interview with Larimer County. The position which was open was a half-time Alcohol Evaluation Specialist. For the second interview, I did exactly what I shared with you above. After the interview, Chief Probation Officer John Elliott told me to call him at 2 PM that afternoon. I told my friend and roommate Mike Pettit, who drove me to the interview, that I thought the job was mine. Well, I was correct!

When I started, I was told that I would be given some interns from Colorado State University to assist me. The caseload which I inherited was over 350 people and very disorganized. While I did receive some formal training on assessing treatment recommendations for DUI/DWAI offenders about six months later, I was given a three ringed notebook with outlined criteria indicators for the type of treatment the individual would need. I can still remember my first intern, Dan Knab and we just clicked right away. The problem I was having in the beginning was I had other interns who would fail to show up or had prior commitments with school. I ended up taking control of the situation by asking an old church friend, Sandra Keefer to help me out and get my feet on the ground. While this worked for a period of time, I knew that I needed to do something different to maintain employment. As shared with you earlier, my father, Jim Mueller, had an employment service called ACIM Personnel Service where he would find people employment. The primary focus of the business was accounting, clerical, industrial and management [hence ACIM] positions. I asked him if I hired my own clerical assistant, could he take care of the Federal and State taxes associated with my hired help. He generously agreed to do so and I would pay the business once a month. Another divine intervention from God! I can recall the first two people I hired were Cathy VerStraeteen and Kimberly Eberhardt. I also had Sandra Keefer continue to work for me. Kimberly and Cathy served as my Clerical Assistant for the next 2 and 6½ years respectively. Again, I continue to be blessed by divine intervention over and over. I worked well with both, however, I must say Cathy's strong commitment and dedication was amazing! Thinking back, she really taught me how to treat my clients with dignity and respect. Over time I began to gain the respect of both the District and County Court for the 8th Judicial District. In the Spring of 1993, a Mr. Tim Walsh was hired as the Chief Probation Officer from Steamboat Springs, Colorado. After getting to know him and what made him tick, he changed the culture of the district into an empowering environment for his employees. He truly exemplified a positive work environment and trusted every employee with their skill set. For me personally, I knew he trusted me and a got to the point where I would go through the wall [figuratively speaking of course] for him. Truly, truly an honest straightforward man with a great sense of humor. To this day, we are still extremely close friends. He has a heart for people and their well-being. To be honest with you, when the State Judicial System first began practicing restorative justice principles, Mr. Walsh was at the forefront and a great example for all of us to follow. Another divine intervention from God. Several years later, I approached Mr. Walsh about the need to provide "reasonable accommodations" under the Americans with Disabilities Act. We together began to brainstorm what State Judicial needed to do. I told him about the new computer software called Dragon Dictate. About three years earlier the State Judicial Branch had switched from typewriter or handwritten documents to computer software. The powers that be within the State Judicial Branch agreed and upgraded/installed the software into my computer. Of course, they also had to integrate the telephone into my system.

The State also hired an independent contractor to train me on the new software system. Looking back, by the grace of God, I became a pioneer for the State Judicial Branch. By this, I hope I have opened some new doors and broadened the scope of the State Judicial Branch to hire other disabled people with the same aspirations and goals. In February 2000, my assistant was hired as a Probation Officer for Larimer County. The irony of the whole story was several years later she became my supervisor. Consequently, we already had a great relationship and I always wanted to put my best foot forward. There is an important side note to this story which I would like to share. At the time, I had a caretaker whose name is Marsha Inskeep whom I became extremely close to. Upon Cathy's departure, I was having difficulty finding a replacement. Marsha only had Certified Nurse Aide experience and never had any clerical assistant experience whatsoever. Over time I began to understand how to manage a caseload and how to communicate with different treatment agencies in conjunction with how the Court system worked. We worked together for the next 23 years and were a great team together! I also saw great personal growth and great personal confidence in what she could accomplish.

Marsha, I want to personally thank you for your dedication

and commitment to me. I also want to the 8th Judicial District for recognizing your dedication and service. Additionally, Marsha gained the trust of the Court with your communication and knowledge base as to what the Court was requesting or exactly was needed at the time. On their behalf, I want to also thank you.

At this point, I would like to expand on the definition of restorative justice. First, I need to give you some case history. In 1995, the Larimer County Probation Department established a Vision Statement which coincided with the State Court Administrative Office own visionary practices. The 8th Judicial Probation Department original vision statement went as follows: 1] Provide a positive supporting, empowering, caring atmosphere. 2] Contributing to an environment which effectively meets client and staff needs. 3] Recognizing, utilizing and valuing the diverse qualities of individuals. 4] Promoting positive change in clients. Personally, I embraced these practices and had been doing so since I was hired in November

1992. Basically, as my parents had taught me: "Treat People by The Golden Rule." As I'm sure most of you know this means to "Treat People the Way You Want to Be Treated." This follows right along with Scripture, specifically Luke 6:31 "Also, just as you want men to do to you, do the same way to them. "Another Scripture which exemplifies restorative justice is from Micah 6:8 which reads "He has shown me, O man, what is good and want the Lord required of you; do justice, love mercy and walk humbly with God." Throughout my career, especially as a Probation Officer, it is of utmost importance to connect with people right where they are at, whether it be good or bad. The key is to listen with intention, which opens the door to compassion, understanding and trust. Then when this foundation is established people become more open, and vulnerable to being held accountable. These types of relationships are only accomplished over an extended period which allows the relationship to prosper. All of us, no matter what road we have traveled, need to know that we are valued and are of utmost importance. The use of humor is a great way to help build a relationship. To be lighthearted and to have people feel safe to open up. They want to get to know you better I have learned is there are times when appropriate, my mind is thinking "How can I put a positive spin on this to laugh wholeheartedly or just with a little chuckle." I purposely did this every day in my professional career, to create a personal connection. As a result, after a period of time, the clientele I was working with didn't even see my wheelchair and I believe that some could not wait to see me to discuss their accomplishments and yes, even their struggles. At this juncture, I want to share with you on several occasions over the course of my career, the people who were on my caseload

At this point in the book, I want to share with you some other great life experiences. These experiences coincide with other great friendships which have grown and prospered over the years. Earlier in the book, I talked about my close friends, Jon and Monique Thompson. In 2004, our church [Summitview Community Church] went to

Yellowstone National Park in Wyoming. The point I wanted to make was Jon volunteered to take care of me while we were on the trip. Several other people also humbly offered to help. While on the trip, Jon and I really had an opportunity to see God's great glory and magnificent creation. On the way there, I can remember having some real heartfelt laughter and that it was just contagious! Additionally, the glaciers, mountains, buffaloes, deer and other wildlife was just amazing. Let me profess to you that when people openly volunteer to take care of your personal needs, you get the opportunity to see real discipleship firsthand. The interesting part is when all the barriers are down, they see how I handle and manage life where there is nothing to hide. Over time we become more open and can share our dreams, aspirations, feelings, disappointments and other emotions. During this trip, I became closer to Jon, Monique and the family. At this point, I consider Jon to be a brother and I know that I am a part of their family. I feel just as close to his wife Monique, who is his sister to me. As a result, I have also become close to Jon's brother, Brick and his wife Stacy. Thank you all for letting me into your life.

Another recent opportunity came in March 2021. My good friends, Mike and Edie Sweezy invited me to go to Hawaii with them to celebrate their 25th anniversary together. Who does that? Anyway, a great opportunity! It will be something I will never forget! We stayed on the Island of Oahu and it was just beautiful. Upon our arrival, we stayed with a friend of Mike's, Dave, who was very generous. Let me just say, I was in awe and amazement during the whole trip. From the airport, Dave drove us up and around Oahu, near one of the volcanoes and up into what I thought of was like a jungle. They had what was called these Monkey Trees that hung so low it looks like you could touch them as we drove by in his Jeep. On the first day, Mike, Edie and myself decided to go and tour the Dole Pineapple Plantation. The flowers and plants there were just so vibrant, colorful, more than you can ever imagine. The pineapples were amazing. It caused my taste buds that have this amazing taste explosion that I have never experienced before.

On the second day, we went to Pearl Harbor. What a humbling and amazing experience. To see all the military service men and women who passed away was extremely humbling. I can remember just sitting there and looking at all the names. I could have just sat there for hours and been just fine. It made me think of my father who served in the Korean War. What a great service to mankind. I can remember my father telling me he could have been a career serviceman. During his life span, I believe he felt this was his most important calling. On the lighter side, if he had stayed, he would never have met my mother, and I or my brothers would have never been a twinkle in his eye.

On the third day, I had an opportunity of a lifetime. My buddy, Mike, made arrangements for the three of us to go up in a helicopter on a guided tour. What an experience. Let me start off by telling you I had 4-5 people carry me up about 6 stairs up into the helicopter. That in and of itself was one of the biggest challenges. It is something that is beyond explanation. I think we were able to see a majority, if not all the islands.

On the fourth day, we all went on a guided sailboat ride on the Pacific Ocean. What an amazing experience. To feel the Ocean breeze and warm wind against your face was very refreshing and soothing. I felt like all the cares of the world had been washed away nothing else mattered. That evening, we went to a Luau called Paradise Cove that was just amazing. The most amazing part of show were the dancers who would throw flaming torches in the air as part of their performance.

On the last couple days of the trip, Mike made arrangements to stay at a quaint little residence on a Naval Base. While there, Mike found out we could rent a beach wheelchair that floated on the water. I must admit I was very apprehensive at first, however, once I got into the ocean it was incredible! As the old Beach Boys song goes, I was "Surfing USA" baby! Thanks again Mike and Edie for an experience of a lifetime, it will be a memory I will never, never forget.

Let me take this opportunity to tell you more about growing up in the Mueller household. My father was serious when he needed to be, however, a real kid at heart his whole life. As for my brothers, Todd and Troy, they both are very close to me and they are supportive of each other. They always included me in their activities both inside and outside our home growing up. Several of my fondest memories were walking down to Datino's restaurant at University Hills Shopping Center for pizza. This usually occurred on Thursday's when my mother was playing golf at Kennedy or Wellshire Golf Course. I can also remember playing basketball at our next neighbor's residence with my brother Todd. We would play the game H.O.R.S.E. or P.I.G. and I would use my imagination to make the most difficult shot. Of course, I could not shoot myself and my brother would shoot for me. In the back of my mind, I knew he could probably make the first shot, however, I knew he could not make the same shot twice in a row. He however proved me wrong a lot of the time. Let me tell you more about my brother Todd. As I stated before, both of my brothers were very athletic. On more than one occasion, Todd would tell me, even when he was playing Varsity sports in both basketball and baseball at Thomas Jefferson High School, he was playing on my behalf since I could not. Talk about touching my heart! Oh my God! Those conversations I have with you will never be forgotten and will be cherished for the rest of my life. Thank you!

Another fond memory was when we would play basketball in the back family room. We used to have a small basketball hoop which you could put up against a plate glass window. Well as the story goes, we had a sliding door with a plate glass window which went out to a covered patio. Well, I was about 15 or 16 years old and I had my first power wheelchair. Well, I was playing defense and my brother took a shot. As I was turning around to get the rebound, my wheelchair shattered the plate glass window. As soon as it happened, I started crying because I knew I was in serious trouble. As I recall, neither of our parents were home at the time, so my mother was the first to hear the rendition of what happens. Naturally, she was initially upset and I was more concerned about how my father would react once he got home from work. I think she however forewarned him ahead of time and he also was initially upset, however, a few hours later we all began to laugh about it.

.

My brothers also played football on the side of the house where there was a good-sized yard. They would invite the neighborhood boys to play football after school. I would sit on the makeshift sidelines and watch them play. Whenever possible, they made sure that I was there participating in whatever activity. What a blessing! As we have gotten older, I have seen the wisdom and knowledge they both have and how they have shared it with me. Granted, we may not agree on everything, however, I know that we love and respect each other. This is most important in all family relationships! This really played out in February 2020 and August 2022. The first incident in February, I was taken to the hospital due to some bleeding in my esophagus. I really listened to what they had to tell me and heeded their advice. This was especially true of my middle brother Todd, who had been recently hospitalized himself. Most recently in August 2022, I was hospitalized for one week with cellulitis. My brother Troy at the time was on vacation in Colorado from Washington, DC, and he came up almost every day from Denver to visit me in the hospital. My sister-in-law Carla also came to see me a couple times while I was in the hospital. Additionally, my brother Todd would call me every other day to see how I was doing. My other sister-in-law Billie, even though I did not see her, I knew in my heart that I was in her thoughts and prayers.

With both Todd and Troy, I can remember playing football with him again in the family room. How we would play, he would place my manual wheelchair in front center of the couch. The couch was the end zone. Of course, I was on the defensive side of the ball and we would play [let me clarify, I would play] goal line defense. Troy would try to literally mow me over or try and jump over me into the end zone. It was amazing that I didn't first get hurt and secondly that our mother allowed this to happen. Looking back on it now, my mother probably thought that this was a good way to connect with them.

At this time, I would like to say more about my dear friend, Marsha Inskeep. I first met Marsha in 1999. She started out by being my health care taker and our relationship grew from there. Marsha is a beautiful wonderful person who has a God-given gracious heart. Her first priority is having Christ in the center of her heart and to be a servant unto Him. Secondly, to be a servant unto others, just as Christ was a servant while here on earth. I have seen this repeatedly in 30 years that I have known her. Whenever I was in need or needed someone to lean on or just talked to, she has always been there for me. Whenever I was in the hospital, she has always been there for me, looking out for my own best interest. People say that "we are like an old married couple," which I am okay with, and am honored to be thought of and considered in that fashion. I know then she has the heart of Christ, which I do also. Marsha's real heart is to help the downtrodden, specifically to feed the hungry and help the homeless. Her real desire is to have a have a food truck, to help the homeless who have a desire to remain clean and sober and to have a personal relationship with our Lord and Savior Jesus Christ. Through the years, I have seen her grow spiritually demanding more and more on her own personal walk with Jesus Christ. As a result, even though my own personal walk is very strong, watching her depending on her faith is an inspiration. I love you my dear friend!

There is another family which I am extremely close to, who I want acknowledge at this time. They are Josh and Kelli Hill, Connor and Caitlin Schultz, Collin and Skyler Schultz, McKenna Schultz and Macy Schultz. First, I met Kelli in 1991 when she first moved to Greeley, Colorado with her first husband Casey. Kelli is a bundle of joy, where you can see the light of Jesus in her eyes and heart. She is fun-loving, full of laughter, where people are naturally drawn towards her. She has done an amazing job raising all her children [now adults] how to embrace Jesus into their hearts and how to love each other. I am truly honored to be considered a part of the family. Her current husband and lifelong companion Josh is truly the salt of the earth. I see him as a rock-solid man who wears Jesus' sandals every day. He is a man who is very firm in his convictions, however, is always willing to listen with open ears and a kind Christ like heart. Kelli is a schoolteacher for children, where God specifically placed her to help mold them with motivation, encouragement and yet provide structured discipline when needed.

As for Connor and Caitlin they are a wonderful couple. Just this last year they had a boy named Micah. The biblical meaning for Micah is poor and humble. Both Connor and Caitlin exemplify this by constantly and continuously being aware of other people's needs before their own. Caitlin said that having a son made their life complete. I will check with them after they have two or three more children, when both parents are going several directions at once. Ha, Ha!

Regarding Collin, we really connected first off in talking about sports. We would both analyze plays either on the football field or basketball court. We would also banter back and forth on player/personnel moves between teams and whether it was a good move one bad move. This, however, does not even scratch the surface of who Collin is as a person or what he is about. Collin is also rock solid in his own spiritual Christian convictions, he is a kind, gentle soul who genuinely cares for people and their well-being. In my lifetime over the last 64 years, I have found this is the best trait a human being should have or possess in their toolbox. Collin, by the grace of God and his willingness to surrender, already has this in his own toolbox.

The next person is McKenna Schultz. McKenna is a great example of God's heart. By this I mean, she is willing to jump in and help head first anyway possible! I have seen firsthand that she has a servant like heart. More specifically, I have seen her with her mother assist with cooking at big family gatherings, listen intently to her siblings and help with whatever is needed at the time. McKenna is also very strong with Scripture and knows her source of strength is in Christ and God the Almighty!

The last however not the least is Macy Schultz. To depict and predicate who Macy is, I need to draw a picture. Macy is pure at heart, joyful and her fun-loving appetite is contagious. People including myself, have been around her when she exudes a playfulness that just consumes who Macy is as a person. She is great with children and knows how to connect and relate to them. Sometimes I think we get caught up in being or responding like an adult and we forget to have a playful, carefree, throw our cares to the wind type attitude. Life is a gift from God Himself and He wants us to enjoy all the gusto of life. Macy truly possesses this in her own life and is an example for us all to follow. Thank you, Macy, I truly have a special place in my heart for you!

As I write this section of the book, there are many other people who have impacted my life that I have not mentioned, however, have been very influential in my life. For those, I want you to know that I have been truly blessed. You all are important in my life and continue to be guideposts of how to live as Christ- like as possible. Granted we all will never reach that pinnacle and it is only by Christ and God's grace that we will enter the gates of heaven and experience the utmost of joy, more than we can ever imagine or understand. May God grant you joy, exuberance for life, peace, fellowship and understanding.

Chapter VI

Spiritual Growth with Intention

I want to start by sharing some Scripture and how I have continued to face my own challenges. Hopefully, by the grace of God, I can convey this by using Scripture in conjunction with my own life. As I have stated previously, most of the time I don't even think about being disabled. That being said, I understand the stark reality each and every day. Let me take this opportunity to explain. I require personal care to meet my basic needs every day. Consequently, I have trained myself how and when it's time to take care of myself. Sometimes, as well as we take care of ourselves, we are thrown a curveball which is unplanned or unexpected. It is then when Scripture states in First Thessalonians 5:18, "Give Thanks in All Situations." Really? You've got to be kidding! Yes, this is true. Let me explain further. A friend of mine, who was in a wheelchair, explained to me that despite the situation we are in at the time, that this too shall pass and I will be able to move on in a couple of hours. Bingo! Ever since then, I have developed this mindset! Praise God! This was even true when I was hospitalized. In the meantime, I needed to pray His for grace and understanding of my emotions I am feeling at the time. I can honestly say this is true! He meets me right where I am at and totally understands my emotions at the time. Recently, I have found a statement by Author CS Lewis which I believe coincides with this thought process. He wrote: A fallen man is not only an imperfect creature who needs improvement: He is a rebel who must lay his arms down. To me, this means "" to let go and let God." This is so hard to do, because as human beings we are brought up and trained to take control of situations in adulthood. For clarification purposes, this does not mean taking care of our responsibilities. That is why God gave us the gift of a brain to think things through with good old common sense. By the same token, it means that we have control over nothing and, in turn, surrender to Him and enjoy the fruits of the Spirit which are love, peace, forbearance, kindness, goodness, gentleness and self-control [Galatians 5:22-23], which He has given us.

Secondly, I/we need to hold steadfast in our Christian faith, as Scripture tells us in 1 Peter 4:12-13 "And now, dear friend of mine, I beg you not to be unduly alarmed at the fiery ordeals of your faith as though this were some abnormal experience. You should be glad, because it means that you are called to share Christ's sufferings. One day, when He shows Himself in full splendor of men, you will be filled with tremendous joy. When I look at my own life, I need to first be thankful for the life that God has given to me. I also need to be thankful and grateful for the numerous opportunities he has given me to impact so many different people. I truly believe God has given me a divine thought process to really listen to help others. Along the same lines, author Ralph Waldo Emerson wrote: Never lose an opportunity of seeing anything beautiful, for the beauty is in God's handwriting.

Thinking back, I recall many conversations I had with both of my parents where I was told if I began to feel downtrodden or sorry for myself, I needed to give myself away. This meant to find someone who was in need. Consequently, I began to think of other people's needs rather than dwelling on myself and it worked. That is exactly what Jesus did when he was here on earth. This is the foundation of restoration of others and the platform that I firmly stand on. If you are unsure where God is directing you then watch, wait and listen. This means utilizing God's discernment, to keep a keen eye on what is exactly needed. This also means that we need to wait patiently to listen and hear exactly what God is telling us to do and what direction we are to go. A lot of the time, we may need to wait to hear the direction God wants us to go. To do this, the Bible tells us to pray unceasingly to hear what He is telling us. Personally, I cannot tell you how frequently this has occurred in my own life. There have been times when I have been in a situation, circumstance or conversation where I have gone to God directly for guidance. More often than not, God has led my speech as well as my thought process while I am in a situation or circumstance. More recently, since I retired, I've had to wait to hear the next endeavors He wants me to take on. To be honest, this has been a real challenge. Personally, I have always handled or tackled situations head on. This was especially true in the workplace. For the last 30 years, there was always something that I needed to handle for that particular day. Additionally, there was always the unexpected situations which occurred every day. I thrived in this type of environment as a Probation Officer. Since then, the journey has been a battle within myself in discovering what God has planned and waiting for what doors He will open. In reality, it has taken me over 1.5 years to find God's new purpose and direction. The problem I faced after retiring was that I am a very social being. I now spend more time alone awaiting God's plan and yet I am still very active in volunteering my time with mentoring youth who are still in high school, the Restorative Justice Program with the City of Fort Collins, as well as being a bench coach for boys' basketball at Liberty Commons High School for both the JV and Varsity teams. All the above stated activities are great and I thoroughly enjoy. Also, in writing this book, there have been times when I have been very encouraged in documenting what God has revealed to me and sharing this with others. Praise God!

Let me share a thought that I truly believe in and attest too. Having the disability of Cerebral Palsy and still have all my mental capabilities is a true miracle and blessing from God. What a battle tested testimony! By the grace of God, I will continue to run the race for His glory. To be physically healed is not what God desires. The real story occurs when there is healing of the heart and soul. This is true restoration. God is connected with His children, when I am open and admit to Him my struggles, weaknesses, strengths, and questions about life, He is right there, through His Son and our Savior Jesus Christ. My soul is what counts and nothing else matters. Praise Jesus! This coincides with Scripture, specifically Titus 3: 4-5 which states: When God our Savior revealed His kindness and love, He saved us, not only because of the righteousness things we have done, but because of His mercy, He washed out our sins, giving us a new birth and new life through the Holy Spirit. Furthermore, in Isaiah 5-6 it is written: I am the Lord, there is no other besides me, there is no other God, I equip you, though you do not know me, they might know from the rising sun and from the West, that' there is no other besides Me: I am the Lord and there is no other. Consider these struggles and questions as if we are honored. I recently found another quotation which stated: "Remember to wake up every day and to be grateful." Author Unknown. To wear His sandals on our feet is a true honor. In my own life, I am convinced and convicted that this is true and it is only then that I can truly experience His true joy! Missionary and Author Corrie Ten

Boon once wrote: Happiness isn't something that depends on our surroundings; it's something we make inside ourselves. This does not happen overnight or the next day. This happens over a period and there is no timeframe. Everything is in God's time. While we are waiting, we need to keep on going, pray [I personally call this a conversation] fervently and Jesus will anoint your spirit/soul giving you peace and understanding. This, in turn, will give you a sense of purpose and direction. In closing, I would like to share a few quotes, as well as a particular Scripture. They are as follows:

1: Life is short. We spend so much time sweating the small stuff; worrying, complaining, gossiping, comparing, wishing, wanting and waiting for something bigger and better instead of focusing on all the blessings that surround us every day. Life is so fragile and all it takes is a single moment to change everything you take for granted. Focus in on what's important and be grateful that you are blessed! Author Terri Cullun.

2: Remember to wake up every day and be grateful. Author Unknown. For myself, I try to think about what goal or what do I need to accomplish today. This helps me to keep motivated and to be thankful for every day.

3: Sometimes knowledge is too handy. You cannot bear it. In those times, your Heavenly Father will carry you. Author Corrie Ten Boom This is so true and so hard to do sometimes, especially with the loss of someone we deeply cared for and loved. He can handle, understands anything and everything! More specifically, in Matthew 11:28-30 Jesus said: "Come to Me, all who are weary and heavy laden, and I will give you rest. Take my yoke and lean on Me, for I am gentle and humble at heart and you will find rest for your souls. For my yoke is easy and my burden is light". Therefore, don't be afraid to express your anger or your emotions to the Almighty God, for He understands everything we are going through. For He gave His only righteous Son in order to understand what we are experiencing in real life.

4: When you choose joy, you feel good, and when you feel good, you do good, it reminds others of what joy feels like and it just might inspire them to do the same. Cartoonist and Author Charles Schultz. Speaking from experience, this is so true. More specifically, in my professional career, I cannot tell you how important it was to maintain a positive, genuine attitude to connect with people. This is the connection that we all yearn for, to feel validated and valued. In turn, by having a good attitude creates an attraction which draws people towards you. Furthermore, I cannot tell you how many times people have asked me, "How do you have such a positive attitude all the time?" It is only by the grace of God and realizing how blessed and fortunate I am.

5: Why wish upon a star when you can pray to the One who created them. Cartoonist and Author Charles Schultz.

6: The greatest gift you can give someone is your time. Because when you give your time, you are freely investing in someone else's well-being. Author Unknown.

When we actually take the time to think about this, it is the best gift we can give each other. Praise God!

7: One last step and yet the most important. May The Lord bless you and keep you; the Lord make His face shine upon you and be gracious to you: the Lord turn His face toward you and give you peace. Numbers 6:24-26. Thank you!

Made in the USA
Las Vegas, NV
28 July 2024

93036187R10056